D0593814

To _____

From _____

Other giftbooks in the same series by Helen Exley:
Missing You ...   Bon Voyage
Sisters ...   When Love is Forever
True Love ...   For a Good Friend

Published simultaneously in 1996 by Exley Publications in Great Britain, and
Exley Giftbooks in the USA.
Copyright © Helen Exley 1996

12 11 10 9 8 7 6 5 4 3 2

Border illustrations by Juliette Clarke
Edited and pictures selected by Helen Exley

ISBN 1-85015-793-6

Designed by Pinpoint Design.
Picture research by Image Select, London.
Typeset by Delta, Watford.

Printed in China

Exley Publications Ltd, 16 Chalk Hill, Watford, Herts. WD1 4BN.
Exley Giftbooks, 232 Madison Avenue, Suite 1206, NY 10016, USA.

WOMEN'S THOUGHTS

QUOTATIONS SELECTED BY
*H*ELEN EXLEY

EXLEY
NEW YORK · WATFORD, UK

The woman is not needed to do man's work. She is not needed to think man's thoughts.... Her mission is not to enhance the masculine spirit, but to express the feminine; hers is not to preserve a man-made world, but to create a human world by the infusion of the feminine element into all of its activities.

MARGARET SANGER,
FROM *"WOMAN AND THE NEW RACE"*

For women to put our hopes and desires
into words is still a magical
and rebellious thing in spite of how
common it may seem to be.
To have the freedom to push our ideas
and words further than they have
in the past is a gift many women before
us have not been able to savor
(and many still cannot).

JEWELLE GOMEZ

A SENSE OF SELF

A liberated woman is one who feels confident in herself, and is happy in what she is doing. She is a person who has a sense of self.... It all comes down to freedom of choice.

BETTY FORD, b.1939

True emancipation begins neither at the polls nor in courts. It begins in woman's soul.

EMMA GOLDMAN, FROM *"THE TRAGEDY OF WOMEN'S EMANCIPATION"*

A woman cannot meet adequately the
needs of those who are nearest to her if she
has no interests, no friends, no
occupations of her own.

ELEANOR ROOSEVELT (1884-1962)

The woman is greater than the wife and
mother, and in consenting to take upon
herself these relationships she should never
sacrifice one iota of her individuality.

ELIZABETH CADY STANTON (1815-1902)

To be today's real woman, you need to have the physique of Venus, the cunning of Cleopatra, the courage of Joan of Arc, the wardrobe of Marie Antoinette, and the cleaning ability of Ammonia D.

JOYCE JILLSON

Social science affirms that a woman's place in society marks the level of civilization.

ELIZABETH CADY STANTON (1815-1902)

Religion, science, art, economics, have all needed the feminine flavor; and literature, the expression of what is permanent and best in all of these, may be gauged by any time to measure the strength of the feminine ingredient.

ANNA JULIA COOPER

I have met brave women who are exploring the outer edge of human possibility, with no history to guide them, and with a courage to make themselves vulnerable that I find moving beyond the words to express it.

GLORIA STEINEM, b.1934,
FROM *"MS."*, APRIL 1972

I don't know why it should surprise people women are so tough. What I do is probably not as tough as [being] a single mother, raising two kids and paying rent or a mortgage.

LIBBY RIDDLES
(SLED-DOG RACE WINNER)

WE NEED EVERY HUMAN GIFT and
cannot afford to neglect any
gift because of artificial barriers of sex or
race or class or national origin.

MARGARET MEAD (1901-1978),
FROM *"MALE AND FEMALE"*

We women suffragists have a great
mission – the greatest mission
the world has ever known. It is to free half
the human race, and through that
reason to save the rest.

EMMELINE PANKHURST (1857-1928)

I think we have a long way to go in women's rights, in changing and enforcing laws, and in protecting women. I won't think women are successful politically until at least half of all the elected offices are held by women; until half the legal profession is populated by women lawyers; until half of *every* occupation is populated by women – women at all levels, not just at the bottom level; until women are assuming their fair share of responsibility at home but not more. We have a long way to go.

GLORIA ALLRED

As a woman presenter, give your listeners a sense of perspective, a sense of a woman, a person, who is imperfect but competent; one who is imperfectable, knows it, and can laugh at it. Be a woman. Be a real person. That's all you have to be.

CAROLYN WARNER,
FROM "THE LAST WORD"

When will women begin to have the first glimmer that above all other loyalties is the loyalty to truth, i.e., to yourself, that husband, children, friends, and country are as nothing to that?

ALICE JAMES

WHAT MAKES A SUCCESSFUL BUSINESSWOMAN?
Is it talent? Well, perhaps, although I've known
many enormously successful people
who were not gifted in any outstanding way, not
blessed with particular talent. Is it, then,
intelligence?… What, then, is the
mystical ingredient? It's persistence. It's that
certain little spirit that compels
you to stick it out just when you're at your most
tired. It's that quality that forces
you to persevere, find the route around the stone
wall. It's the immovable stubbornness
that will not allow you to cave in when everyone
says give up.

ESTEE LAUDER, b.1908,
FROM "ESTEE: A SUCCESS STORY"

*To be somebody, a woman does
not have to be more like a man, but has to be
more of a woman.*

SALLY E. SHAYWITZ, b.1942

*Womankind holds at its heart the
understanding that love, not power, ensures the
continuance of life.
Each woman holds the hope of reconciliation, of
sanity, of peace, of strength in kindness,
of humankind discovering it is one family.*

PAM BROWN, b.1928

In all the world there cannot be another plane quite like the official jet of the Prime Minister of Pakistan, Benazir Bhutto. The front section is a kind of office-cum-nursery, jammed with toys, briefcases, newspapers, nannies and Bhutto's children, Bilawal, 5, Bakhtawar, 4, and Asifa, 1. In the main cabin, political advisers, security commandos

and generals are keeping an eye on the
Prime Minister they cautiously support.
"Hello, gentlemen... Hello, babies,"
Bhutto calls as she enters the plane.
It is both jarring and interesting to see
soldiers saluting a woman with children
on her lap.

CLAUDIA PREIFUS,
FROM *"THE NEW YORK TIMES
MAGAZINE"*, MAY 13, 1994

Woman is shut up in a kitchen or in a boudoir, and astonishment is expressed that her horizon is limited. Her wings are clipped, and it is found deplorable that she cannot fly.

SIMONE DE BEAUVOIR (1908-1986), FROM *"THE SECOND SEX"*

Protectiveness has often muffled the sound of doors closing against women.

BETTY FRIEDAN, b.1921, FROM *"THE FEMININE MYSTIQUE"*

Women have a certain relationship to their presence on the planet which is, I suspect, to do with their potential to bear children or the fact that they have borne children, which roots them in a sounder way to the purpose of life.... They seem to understand their own natures, they listen to their bodies and they're not in flight from themselves.

JOAN BAKEWELL, b.1933,
FROM *"WOMEN"* BY NAIM ATTALLAH

Woman knows what man has long
forgotten, that the ultimate economic and

spiritual unit of any civilization
is still the family.

CLARE BOOTHE LUCE (1903-1987)

When women are supposed to be quiet, a talkative woman is one who talks at all.

DALE SPENDER

A man has to be Joe McCarthy to be called ruthless. All a woman has to do is put you on hold.

MARLO THOMAS, b.1943

Man forgives woman anything save the wit to outwit him.

MINNA ANTRIM

Failing to be there when a man wants her is a woman's greatest sin, except to be there when he doesn't want her.

HELEN ROWLAND (1875-1950)

What would happen if one woman told the truth about her life? The world would split open.

MURIEL RUKEYSER (1913-1980)

A woman should, I think, love her husband better than anything on earth except her own soul, which I think a man should respect above everything on earth but his own soul; and there my dear is a very pretty puzzle for you, which a good many people have failed to solve.

FANNY KEMBLE (1809-1893)

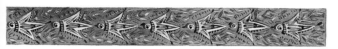

We have won the right to be terminally exhausted.

ERICA JONG, b.1942

The economic dependence of women is perhaps the greatest injustice that has been done to us, and has worked the greatest injury to the race.

NELLIE MCCLUNG (1873-1961),
FROM "IN TIMES LIKE THESE"

And woman should stand beside man as the comrade of his soul, not the servant of his body.

CHARLOTTE PERKINS GILMAN (1860-1935)

As women we must keep up our courage. Even though Susan B. Anthony had been struggling to win the right to vote and it wasn't achieved in her lifetime, her final words on her deathbed were, "Failure is impossible." It takes a great deal of courage for women to survive what they have to endure, because they are second-class citizens, subordinated, taken advantage of, betrayed... treated with little dignity and respect.

Women must have courage. That's what is needed. They should stand up, speak out, and fight back.

GLORIA ALLRED
FROM "ON WOMEN TURNING 50"

RASPBERRIES!

I REFUSE TO CONSIGN the whole male sex to the nursery. I insist on believing that some men are my equals.

BRIGID BROPHY

Women speak because they wish to speak, whereas a man speaks only when driven to speech by something outside himself – like, for instance, he can't find any clean socks.

JEAN KERR

When God made man she was having one of her off days.

GRAFFITI

The practice of putting women on pedestals began to die out when it was discovered that they could give orders better from that position.

BETTY GRABLE (1915-1973)

A guy is a lump like a doughnut. So, first you gotta get rid of all the stuff his mum did to him, and then you gotta get rid of all that macho crap that they pick up from the beer commercials. And then there's my personal favourite, the male ego.

ROSEANNE

*M*othering/nurturing is a vital force
and process establishing
relationships throughout the
universe. Exploring and analyzing
the nature of all components
involved in a nurturing
activity puts one in touch with life
extending itself.
This is the feminine presence.
The earth is woman.

BERNICE J. REAGON

I spend a lot of time talking to women and to women's groups trying to convince them that the experiences they've had in life are as valid as any experiences men have had. I think that needs to be said again and again.

CAROLINE HOGG

Don't shut yourself up in a bandbox just because you are a woman, but understand what is going on, and educate yourself to take part in the world's work, for it all affects you and yours.

LOUISA MAY ALCOTT (1832-1888)

Feminism is the most revolutionary idea
there has ever been. Equality for women
demands a change in the human psyche
more profound than anything Marx
dreamed of. It means valuing parenthood
as much as we value banking.

POLLY TOYNBEE,
FROM *"THE GUARDIAN"*, 1987

People call me a feminist whenever I
express sentiments that differentiate me
from a doormat or a prostitute.

REBECCA WEST (1892-1983)

Feminism has become the shorthand for the proclamation that women's experience should become an integral part of what goes into the definition of being human.

MERCY AMBA ODUYOYE

I think that implicit in the women's movement is the idea that women will share in the economic burden, and men will share more equally in the home and the family.

BETTY FRIEDAN, b.1921

The worser effect on both man and woman

is found where woman's acceptance

of insult, having grown mechanical, is

eventually unconscious.

ELIZABETH ROBINS,
FROM "ANCILLA'S SHARE"

Many women have more power than they recognize,

and they're very hesitant to use it, for they

fear they won't be loved.

PATRICIA SCHROEDER

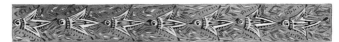

Like an immigrant group out to pull ourselves up by our bootstraps, women may help each other with public speaking, confidence building, solutions to professional problems, announcements of job openings, or lists of women-owned businesses and services to support. Considering our training to look to men for expertise and authority, it's a victory that we now empower each other as professionals by seeking out women physicians and gynecologists (for whom demand now exceeds the supply), women rabbis and ministers for group ceremonies, women audio technicians for our meetings and concerts, women stock analysts for our investments, and women piano tuners,

company plane pilots, security guards, and
carpenters for home or office.
"We're not lowering our standards," said a Houston
woman when challenged on her group's choice of a
woman architect. "We may even be raising them.
Statistically speaking, women professionals had to
be better to get where they are.".... More and more
we're seeing the empowerment of another woman
as a reciprocal gift.

GLORIA STEINEM, b.1934, FROM
"NETWORKING" IN "OUTRAGEOUS ACTS AND
EVERYDAY REBELLIONS"

No One's Gonna Keep Me Down

I am woman, hear me roar.
In numbers too big to ignore
And I know too much to go back and
    pretend
'Cause I've heard it all before
And I've been down there on the floor
And no-one's ever gonna keep me
    down again.

HELEN REDDY AND RAY BURTON

A woman's duty: To look the whole world in the face with a go-to-hell look in the eyes; to have an ideal; to speak and act in defiance of convention.

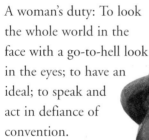

INTERNATIONAL LADIES' GARMENT WORKERS' UNION

The bond between women is a circle – we
are together within it.

JUDY GRAHN

To be equal, we have to become who
we really are and women we never will be equal
women until we love one another woman....

JILL JOHNSTON,
QUOTED IN *"THE SISTERHOOD"*, BY MARCIA COHEN

The woman who has sprung free has emotional mobility. She is able to move toward the things that are

satisfying to her and away from those that are not. She is free, also, to succeed.

COLETTE DOWLING

Women have been abused, misused and
the appendages of men for
centuries, and now we finally have an
opportunity to be ourselves.

JOAN COLLINS, b.1933,
FROM "MY SECRETS"

Nothing on Earth is more gladdening
than knowing we must roll up
our sleeves and move back the boundaries of
the humanly possible once more.

ANNIE DILLARD

Young women have a big task of resisting pressures and challenging definitions. Their increasing success is a miracle of foresight and courage that should make us all proud.

GLORIA STEINEM, b.1934, FROM "NETWORKING" IN *"OUTRAGEOUS ACTS AND EVERYDAY REBELLIONS"*

Who ever walked behind anyone to freedom? If we can't go hand in hand, I don't want to go.

HAZEL SCOTT, FROM *"MS."*, NOVEMBER 1974

Learning moment by moment to be free in our minds and hearts, we make freedom possible for everyone the world over.

SONIA JOHNSON, b.1936

If one burdens the future with one's worries, it cannot grow organically. I am filled with confidence, not that I shall succeed in worldly things, but that even when things go badly for me I shall still find life good and worth living.

ETTY HILLESUM,
FROM *"AN INTERRUPTED LIFE: THE DIARIES OF ETTY HILLESUM"*

My will shall shape my future.
Whether I fail or succeed shall be no man's
doing but my own. I am the force; I can
clear any obstacle before me or
I can be lost in the maze. My choice; my
responsibility; win or lose, only I hold the
key to my destiny.

ELAINE MAXWELL

Acknowledgements: The publishers are grateful for permission to reproduce copyright material. While every effort has been made to trace copyright holders, the publishers would be pleased to hear from any not here acknowledged. GLORIA ALLRED: Extracts from *Women Turning 50*, © Gloria Allred 1993, reprinted by permission of HarperCollins, *Inc.* ANNE MORROW LINDBERGH: Extracts from *Gift from the Sea*, © Anne Morrow Lindbergh 1955, reprinted by permission of Curtis Brown Group, UK. HELEN REDDY and RAY BURTON: "I am Woman", © Helen Reddy and Ray Burton, reprinted by permission of Irving Music, Inc. GLORIA STEINEM: Extracts from "Networking" in *Outrageous Acts and Everyday Rebellions*, © Gloria Steinem 1984, reprinted by permission of Random House, UK.

Picture Credits: Exley Publications is very grateful to the following individuals and organizations for permission to reproduce their pictures: Fine Art Photographic Library (FAP), Superstock (SS), Edimedia (EDI), Scala (SCA), The Bridgeman Art Library (BAL), Statens-Konstmuseer (SKM), Archiv für Kunst (AKG). Cover: © 1996 Savelij Sorine, *Study*